UNPLUGGED ACTIVITIES FOR FUTURE CODERS

BUILD YOUR COMPUTER SECURITY SKILLS

Adam Furgang and Christopher Harris

Illustrations by Joel Gennari

Enslow Publishing
101 W. 23rd Street
Suite 240
New York, NY 10011
USA

enslow.com

Published in 2020 by Enslow Publishing, LLC
101 W. 23rd Street, Suite 240, New York, NY 10011

Copyright © 2020 by Enslow Publishing, LLC.

MAY - '21

Library of Congress Cataloging-in-Publication Data

Names: Furgang, Adam, author. | Harris, Christopher, author. | Gennari, Joel, illustrator.
Title: Build your computer security skills / Adam Furgang and Christopher Harris ; illustrations by Joel Gennari.
Description: New York : Enslow Publishing, 2020. | Series: Unplugged activities for future coders |
Audience: Grades: 5 to 8. | Includes bibliographical references and index.
Identifiers: LCCN 2019000155| ISBN 9781978510654 (library bound) | ISBN 9781978510647 (pbk.)
Subjects: LCSH: Computer security—Juvenile literature. | Computer security—Study and teaching—
Activity programs.
Classification: LCC QA76.9.A25 F86 2020 | DDC 005.8—dc23
LC record available at https://lccn.loc.gov/2019000155

Printed in the United States of America

To Our Readers: We have done our best to make sure all website addresses in this book were active and appropriate when we went to press. However, the author and the publisher have no control over and assume no liability for the material available on those websites or on any websites they may link to. Any comments or suggestions can be sent by email to customerservice@enslow.com.

Image Credits: Character illustrations by Joel Gennari, crossword grid by Adam Furgang and Christine Pekatowski, other art by Christine Pekatowski.

CONTENTS

INTRODUCTION

"Computer code" is a general term used to describe the various computer software languages that allow our personal computers and mobile devices to run. Computer code is used to make apps, web browsers, video games, and computer operating systems. Learning how to code in various software languages can be complex and difficult. The simple activities in this book will help you to begin to think of more complex computer security programming skills without doing any actual programming.

Think of a home. Our homes are private places where we live and store our personal possessions. We protect our homes with locks and keys that secure doors and windows to make it difficult for strangers to break in. Businesses, banks, restaurants, and schools have various types of security measures in place to protect the people and items inside. Alarms and security systems are sometimes used as added deterrents and to alert authorities if a break-in is attempted.

But what about the personal digital information and files we share on the internet with friends and family? How can we keep our emails, texts, photos, and videos safe and secure from the prying eyes of strangers? And what about sensitive information that uniquely identifies us, such as phone numbers, home addresses, birth dates, email addresses, social

security numbers, credit card numbers, and bank account information? How can we keep that information we constantly send out to various websites from our computers and mobile devices safe from hackers and scammers who try to steal our information to try and impersonate us digitally on the internet? What steps can we take to help lessen the risks that exist every time we go online? Data security companies and computer security specialists work continually to stay many steps ahead of hackers and scammers who are always trying to compromise protections and acquire valuable private information.

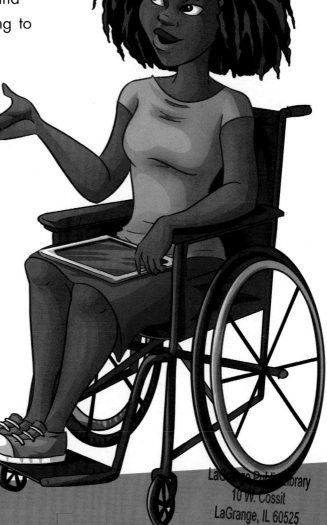

As we do with our real-world homes and possessions, when we use a computer or mobile device, we can use special locks, keys, and security systems to help keep our digital identities and personal information private and secure. With the use of email addresses, birth dates, special security questions that only we know the answers to, and

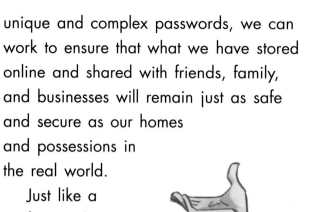

unique and complex passwords, we can work to ensure that what we have stored online and shared with friends, family, and businesses will remain just as safe and secure as our homes and possessions in the real world.

Just like a professional security specialist, you too can learn to build your computer security skills with real-world activities that will get you thinking like a professional security specialist and train your brain for coding in the future. The following unplugged activities require no actual coding or computer—but they will get your mind thinking like a coder. Using mazes, code key puzzles, memory games, binary code keys, scavenger hunts, and other activities, you will begin to consider the internet the same way a professional security specialist might. With sharpened computer security skills, you will be well on your way to a more secure future online.

CAN YOU BREAK THE CODE?

 10–15 minutes

 2+ players

YOUR MISSION

Everyone uses the internet and online technology for so many personal things. When you want to buy something online, you can enter your payment information, buy it, and get your package a few days later! But bad stuff can happen when you give your personal information to a website that is not encrypted—which means it is not keeping your information safe. Encrypted sites use a code so that personal information entered is not viewable by anyone else.

Your Gear

- **Pencil**
- **Paper**

LET'S PLAY

Take a peek at the the three messages on the following page. If you can't read them, don't worry. They're hard to read because they are encrypted! However, it's possible to break an encryption. All you have to do is look at the key, which will tell you which letter corresponds to each symbol in the code.

Using the Can You Break the Code? key, compete with a friend (or a few friends) to see who can decode all three messages the fastest. It's a race, but remember—making mistakes will take you twice as long, so make sure to check your answer!

1. >30 }]~$ 4!33=]@<3 +5!+ 5!10 }0++0@3% ~>890@3% !~< 3289]}37

2. <] ~]+ $^10 !~2]~0 2]>@ 40@3]~!} ^~6]@8!+^]~]~}^~0]@ +5@]>$5 +0[+7

3. <] ~]+ <]=~}]!< !~2 >~*~]=~ 3]6+=!@07

CAN YOU BREAK THE CODE? KEY

Symbol	Letter
!	a
9	b
{	c
<	d
0	e
6	f
$	g
5	h
^	i
&	j
*	k
}	l
8	m
~	n
]	o
4	p
?	q
@	r

Symbol	Letter
3	s
+	t
>	u
1	v
=	w
[	x
2	y
#	z
%	'
7	.

REVIEW YOUR MOVES

• How can you keep your personal information safe online?

• How do your choices or behavior change if you know that a certain website is encrypted?

STRONG PASSWORD ALGORITHM

 10–15 minutes

 1+ players

YOUR MISSION

Everyone has so many passwords nowadays—from Instagram to their personal phones—that it's easy to get caught making a weak one. You might even think, "If I use my birthday, I'll never forget it!" But what if somebody else tried to get into your account? Your birthday might be posted on a wall at school or visible to all your friends on social media. You'd wish you had a stronger password then!

The best passwords have uppercase and lowercase letters, numbers, and symbols. They also don't use a regular word because that would be easy to guess. But how are you supposed to remember all of those? By creating an algorithm—or a set of rules—to follow for making a password, you will be able to create complicated passwords for multiple accounts and never forget them!

Your Gear

- **Pencil**
- **Paper**

LET'S PLAY

Start off by writing down a list of rules that someone can follow to create complex passwords. Here are some questions you can use to guide your rules:

- What words or letters will be in your password?
- How will you decide which numbers to include in your password?
- How will you decide which symbols to include in your password?
- Where are you going to put the letters, numbers, and symbols? Will they be in the same spot for every password? (Example: words, then numbers, then symbols OR words, with symbols in between letters and numbers at the end.)

Once you have this list, you've essentially got an algorithm! Give your list of rules to your friends or parents and have them try to create a complex password using your algorithm. Maybe they'll even think about increasing their personal security!

REVIEW YOUR MOVES

• The tricky thing about a password algorithm is that, if someone finds it, they'll be able to decode all your passwords. How would you keep it safe?

• Why do you think your algorithm will help you be successful in creating and managing many complex passwords?

ALPHANUMERIC PASSWORD MEMORY GAME

 10–20 minutes 2+ players

YOUR MISSION

Play a password memory game! Most websites and social media apps require that you sign in with a username and a unique password. Usually you will need to pick a username and then create a password with a certain amount of different upper and lowercase letters, numbers, and symbols like @, %, &, #. Because remembering a complex password can be difficult, many people often use simple passwords, such as "password" or "123456." Using simple passwords is not a good idea because hackers can easily figure them out and possibly gain access to your account.

Your Gear

- **Pencil**
- **Paper**
- **Index card**

LET'S PLAY

Remembering a complex password with random letters, numbers, and symbols can be difficult, but it can also help keep your internet accounts safe from hackers. Choose a player to go first and start by creating a simple password with three letters.

Keep Them Fresh and New!

Even if you have a strong password that's difficult for a hacker to figure out, it's a good idea to change your passwords frequently. Sometimes large corporations have data breaches and hackers gain access to customers' personal information. Sometimes, that could mean that hackers got hold of millions of people's passwords! But if you frequently change your passwords, any password obtained in a data breach may be outdated by the time someone goes to use it.

The next player in the group will say the password aloud before adding their own additional number, symbol, or letter to the password.

The goal of the game is to remember the increasingly complex password (without writing it down!) as each player adds another number, symbol, or letter to it. Once a player recalls the password incorrectly, he or she is out of the game. The last player left in the game wins.

SYMBOL CHART

! - exclamation point
@ - at symbol
# - hash, pound, or number symbol
$ - dollar sign
% - percent sign
^ - caret
& - ampersand or and symbol
(- open parentheses
) – close parentheses

REVIEW YOUR MOVES

• If you are playing with a large group, have just one person keep track of the password on an index card as it increases in complexity.

• How can you remember many different complex passwords?

• Use the symbol chart on the facing page to learn the names of different symbols you can use in your password.

• Different websites require different number, letter, or symbol combinations. Change the requirements to alter the memory game.

BINARY MESSAGE DECODER

 20–30 minutes

 2 players

YOUR MISSION

Decode a secret message! Computer software languages are made from binary code. A binary code uses only two numbers, 0 and 1. The value of 0 or 1 in binary code is called a bit. It is the smallest unit of measurement used by a computer. For different representations of letters or numbers in binary code, strings of eight bits of 0 or 1 are used to make what is called a byte. There are 256 various possible combinations of 0 and 1 in a byte. A string of eight bits makes up a single byte in binary code. For example, the capital letter A is represented as 01000001 in binary code.

LET'S PLAY

Your Gear

- **Pencil**
- **Paper**

You might think the 0s and 1s on the top of the next page are nothing but gibberish. They are not! They make up a binary message. Each string of eight 0s and 1s is a single byte that represents either a capital letter or a number. Use the binary chart on page 18 to translate the binary message's string of bytes into capital letters and numbers. Then you will be able to decode the message and read what it says.

BINARY MESSAGE

01000010 01001001 01001110 01000001 01010010 01011001
01010101 01010011 01000101 01010011
01001111 01001110 01001100 01011001
00110000
01000001 01001110 01000100
00110001

Now rewrite this same message using a mix of numbers and capital and lowercase letters. Finally use the chart to write a secret message for a friend. Then ask that friend to use the binary chart to decode it!

REVIEW YOUR MOVES

• How can I use binary code to protect my information?

• The 0 and 1 in the chart can be replaced with shapes, such as square and triangle, to make your own binary chart. This will help you to further code your messages. Only you will know which shape represents 0 and which shape represents 1.

• Binary is very common. If you want to make your messages secret, make a new chart and mix up the letters so only friends with the binary chart will be able to translate your binary code.

BINARY CHART

Capital Letters	Lowercase Letters	Numbers
A - 01000001	a - 01100001	0 - 00110000
B - 01000010	b - 01100010	1 - 00110001
C - 01000011	c - 01100011	2 - 00110010
D - 01000100	d - 01100100	3 - 00110011
E - 01000101	e - 01100101	4 - 00110100
F - 01000110	f - 01100110	5 - 00110101
G - 01000111	g - 01100111	6 - 00110110
H - 01001000	h - 01101000	7 - 00110111
I - 01001001	i - 01101001	8 - 00111000
J - 01001010	j - 01101010	9 - 00111001
K - 01001011	k - 01101011	
L - 01001100	l - 01101100	
M - 01001101	m - 01101101	
N - 01001110	n - 01101110	
O - 01001111	o - 01101111	
P - 01010000	p - 01110000	
Q - 01010001	q - 01110001	
R - 01010010	r - 01110010	
S - 01010011	s - 01110011	
T - 01010100	t - 01110100	
U - 01010101	u - 01110101	
V - 01010110	v - 01110110	
W - 01010111	w - 01110111	
X - 01011000	x - 01111000	
Y - 01011001	y - 01111001	
Z - 01011010	z - 01111010	

TWO-STEP VERIFICATION

 10 minutes   2+ players

YOUR MISSION

Play a two-step verification game. Two-step verification is used by many websites as an extra security step to help keep your personal accounts secure, even if someone has your username and password. Accounts that use two-step verification require a username and password and for you to provide your cell phone number. Whenever you sign in, a temporary code is sent directly to your cell phone in the form of a text message. In addition to providing your username and password each time you sign in, you will also physically need your cell phone so that

you can get the temporary code and enter it in a timely fashion to gain access to the website.

LET'S PLAY

Each player will be given an index card with a spot for a username, a password, and a two-step verification code. To get a verification code from another player, each player must make a password to the specifications of the player who will be handing out the code. For example, if you want a verification code from Alex, she will make you follow the password requirements of her choice, such as: "The password you create must be at least 10 characters long, have at least 2 capital letters, have at least 2 lowercase letters, have at least 2 numbers, and have at least 2 symbols." If you want the two-step verification code from another player, you must create the password to that person's specifications. Your partner checks that the password follows the specifications and gives you the verification code if you are correct.

EXAMPLES OF USERNAME, PASSWORD, AND TWO-STEP VERIFICATION CODES

username: JamesJoe	Password: #@936HSWkd	Two-step verification code: 234843
username: SamSmith	Password: 92tyNB&%XX	Two-step verification code: 0064
username: JAX2852	Password: MAN234aa!!	Two-step verification code: 890352

REVIEW YOUR MOVES

• Change the activity by requiring different steps before sending the two-step verification code.

• Some websites require users to answer predetermined personal questions no one else would know. How can you add this extra security measure to authenticate a user's identity and increase security?

• What should a user do if he or she receives a code for a two-step verification but had not attempted to log into a website?

PHISHING FOR INFORMATION

 15–25 minutes   2–6 players

YOUR MISSION

Play a phishing game. Phishing is when hackers and scammers send out phony emails disguised to look like real ones in order to trick you into disclosing your valuable information such as a username and a password, credit cards, or personal information like your birthday or social security number. Links in fraudulent emails will send you to what appears to be a real website. But it's actually designed to fool you into typing your username and password, where it will be collected for criminal purposes.

Your Gear

- **Pencils**
- **Paper clips**
- **String**
- **Index cards**
- **Scissors**

LET'S PLAY

To construct the phishing game, follow these steps:
- Attach a paper clip to an index card so that one half of it is hanging off the side. Bend the paper clip slightly so it will stick up when the index card is placed flat on a surface. Use tape to adhere the paperclip to the index card to secure it. Create five cards with paperclips for each player.

- Create a "phishing hook" by bending a paper clip into a hook shape like the letter "J." Cut the string so it is about two feet long. Attach one end of the string to the pencil with tape and tie the other end to the hook-shaped paper clip. Make the length of the "phishing line" about one foot long. Cut off any excess string.

- Each player fills out the face-down sides of each index card with a paper clip sticking up. They will put make-believe valuable information on one card labeled with their name along with the word "valuable." They will put useless information of the other four cards, such as the day of the week, any color, or a random word.

- Mix all the cards up and be sure they are facing down.

- To play the game, have each player take a single turn and attempt to "phish" for a single card. If a player hooks another player's valuable card, that player is out. Players who hook their own valuable card stay in the game.

- The last player who has not had a valuable card "phished" from the pile wins.

MAKE-BELIEVE VALUABLE INFORMATION CARD EXAMPLES

Do not write real information on the card for this game. Just make up information. You can pretend you are creating a secret identity!

Your Mother's Maiden Name: Morales	Username: JoeSmith	Password: Jhg385&%@119
Date of Birth: 01/04/2008	Your favorite food: Pizza	Cell Phone #: 555-555-5555

REVIEW YOUR MOVES

- How can players make their cards harder to hook?
- How can you avoid being a victim of phishing scams in real life?

Where Are You Now?

Weather apps make extensive use of geolocation services. Users want to know about the weather where they are, so the app needs to figure out the location in order to show an accurate report of current temperatures and conditions. Search engines like Google also use geolocation. The results that you get from Google will differ based on where you are searching from. For mobile users especially, Google wants to show results that are nearby if you are searching for something like a restaurant or hotel. While this is helpful for you as a user, it also means Google can provide more specific ads, based on your location and search terms, which boosts advertising sales. It's all about how these companies can make more money!

WORD SEARCH ENCRYPTED PASSWORD KEY

 10–15 minutes

 1+ players

YOUR MISSION

Solve an encryption puzzle. Encrypted information often requires a key or a code in order to decode the hidden message being sent. Someone who is sent or intercepts an encrypted message will not be able to read it unless they also got hold of the key.

Your Gear

- **Pencil**
- **Graph paper**

LET'S PLAY

Copy the word search on the next page onto graph paper. Circle the hidden words. Then circle the letter that follows each word. (Move in the direction the word is going; if a word reads backwards, the letter will be the one before it.) Unscramble these letters to reveal the secret password.

Then, take it to another level! Create new word searches on graph paper with hidden messages by creating your own secret code for finding hidden letters. See which of you and your friends can build the trickiest encryption key.

WORD SEARCH WORDS AND CHART

encrypt	password	virus
phish	hacker	security
mobile phone	firewall	username

```
k  o  d  b  m  w  e  s  t  u  a  s  c  b  c  m  v
y  r  q  b  x  b  e  s  j  u  a  e  q  s  o  x  s
g  r  s  k  b  d  b  f  s  k  n  c  z  r  h  l  d
j  r  e  s  g  p  s  e  i  o  k  z  d  l  o  w  b
k  x  y  k  s  o  r  j  h  r  a  h  q  f  q  j  s
l  h  l  q  c  n  i  p  u  k  e  o  f  h  n  w  e
m  m  z  q  a  a  e  p  a  s  s  w  o  r  d  r  c
g  x  g  m  e  l  h  x  x  e  w  s  a  f  m  t  u
t  k  e  r  i  i  y  q  k  i  u  e  e  l  s  g  r
j  d  s  b  o  m  n  e  c  c  s  h  g  u  l  i  i
u  m  o  r  l  j  k  o  i  l  j  s  r  n  d  p  t
m  m  c  g  n  j  c  p  n  j  e  i  d  x  j  s  y
n  z  o  g  z  q  m  e  o  c  v  h  s  q  o  f  e
r  z  d  t  p  y  r  c  n  e  t  p  y  i  u  f  m
e  k  v  d  f  x  g  g  t  p  g  d  r  m  a  a  h
n  r  r  c  c  w  f  m  d  k  w  z  p  n  g  s  e
```

REVIEW YOUR MOVES

• Why are encrypted messages more difficult to solve than unencrypted messages?

• What happens if you get one word in the puzzle incorrect?

FINGERPRINT MAZE MOBILE PHONE ACCESS

 30–40 minutes

 2+ players

YOUR MISSION

Make a maze of your own fingerprint. Many computers and mobile devices now use fingerprint readers as an easy and convenient way to securely gain access to our electronic devices without the use of a password. Every person's fingerprint is unique, so the chances of someone else's fingerprint being able to unlock our device is rare. According to Apple, the chance of unlocking a mobile device with an unregistered fingerprint with its Touch ID technology is 1 in 50,000.

Your Gear

- **Pencil**
- **Black marker**
- **Red pencil**
- **Ink pad**
- **Paper**
- **Magnifying glass, copier, or mobile device**

LET'S PLAY

Use the ink pad to ink your index finger. Once your finger has been pressed down evenly in the ink, quickly make an impression of your fingerprint on paper. If it's not clear, try again.

Use your fingerprint as a guide to create a maze with a clear start and finish. Sketch out your maze with a pencil. You can draw it freehand, using a magnifying glass to enlarge the view of your fingerprint. You could also take a picture of your fingerprint with a mobile phone or tablet, enlarge the image on the device screen, and carefully trace it. You could use a copier to blow up the fingerprint and trace that, too. If you need to, add or erase breaks in the lines of the fingerprint to make sure the maze has one—and only one—solution. Then use a black marker to trace the pencil lines.

After each person has created his or her own fingerprint maze, exchange them. Have each player solve the maze with a red pencil. The first person to solve another person's maze wins. Use the example maze to the right to help you get started.

REVIEW YOUR MOVES

• What other technologies use unique physical traits to unlock computers and mobile devices?
• Compare your fingerprints with other players. What are the differences?

MNEMONIC MEMORY PASSWORD PHRASE

 10–15 minutes    *2+ players*

YOUR MISSION

Coming up with a strong password can be tricky. Many websites have their own set of rules for creating a password. It's also a very good idea to never use the same password twice—this way if a website's information is compromised, the hackers can't also get into your account on other websites. And then if you have to change it because of a data breach, you won't need to do it for all of your accounts at once.

Memory tricks can help you remember difficult, hard-to-crack passwords. A mnemonic is a phrase or string of words used to help with memory.

Your Gear

- **Pencil**
- **Index cards**

LET'S PLAY

In this activity you and the other players will come up with a phrase, a favorite book or film quote, or a line from a song to use as a mnemonic. Using the first letters from the phrase, song, or quote, you can generate a strong and secure password that will be quite easy to remember.

Once you have the phrase, quote, or song lines, use the first letter from each word to help you create a secure and easy-to-remember mnemonic password.

For example, you could use *Mary had a little lamb. Its fleece was white as snow.*

Using the first letter of each word from the phrase of the classic nursery rhyme, you could create a password such as: Mh@ LL1fww@S.

Once you have created your password, switch index cards and test each other.

Password Conversions

With some basic rules that you can determine, your mnemonic phrase will always convert certain letters into numbers or symbols. Here are some examples.
- Change "A" to "@"
- Change "I" to "1"
- Change "S" to "5" or "$"

REVIEW YOUR MOVES

- It's a good idea to have some unused mnemonic phrases ready in case you need to change a password after a website has been compromised.
- How can you remember many passwords using a mnemonic phrase? (Hint: Use different lines from the same poem, song, or movie scene for each website.)
- Where can you store your mnemonic phrases and passwords in case you do forget them?

SECURITY SCAVENGER HUNT

 15–20 minutes

 2–4 players

YOUR MISSION

We use our personal information in many different ways with computers and mobile devices. We are often not even aware where our information is going or how it is being transmitted. From cell phone towers to fiber-optic cables to Wi-Fi routers, our personal information and our security often depend on these many forms of quickly changing technology.

Your Gear

- **Pencil**
- **Paper**

LET'S PLAY

Everyone loves a scavenger hunt! You can do this activity at home or school. It will help you and your friends learn about computer security by finding many different types of technology we knowingly or unknowingly use every day.

Go on a scavenger hunt for items that transmit personal information or require personal information to begin using. With many players, pair off into teams. The first person or team to find every item on the list wins. Players will find various computers and mobile, internet, Wi-Fi, cellular, or other technological devices that require security. Start with the list that follows, but add ideas of your own as well. One way to make the scavenger hunt more challenging is to have one player hide old, broken, or unused technology like a Wi-Fi router, old computers discs, and broken cables.

SCAVENGER HUNT LIST

Here are some items you might look for around your classroom, school, or home:

- Desktop or laptop computer
- Mobile phone
- Tablet
- E-reader
- Modem
- Cell tower
- Router
- Hard drive
- Gaming system
- Thumb drive
- Memory card

REVIEW YOUR MOVES

- How can you find out what a device is if you are unsure of its function?
- Make a definition log to keep track of the devices and technology you find to learn about their many uses.

WEB SAFETY REVIEW CROSSWORD PUZZLE

 10–15 minutes   *2–4 players*

YOUR MISSION

Understanding the many words and terms used to improve your computer security skills is important. Practicing smart computer security on the internet will help you begin to think and talk like a computer security professional. Once you know the common terms used by computer security programmers, you will be better prepared to help keep yourself and others safe with computers and the internet.

Your Gear

- **Pencil**
- **Graph paper**

LET'S PLAY

To review the terms used in this book, use the Across and Down clues to help fill in the missing words on the crosssword puzzle on the following page. You can use a pencil and graph paper to copy the crossword puzzle so you do not need to write in the book. Make multiple copies of the puzzle if you want a lot of people to tackle the puzzle at once. Players can work together, or they can compete to see who finishes the puzzle first.

WEB SAFETY REVIEW CROSSWORD PUZZLE

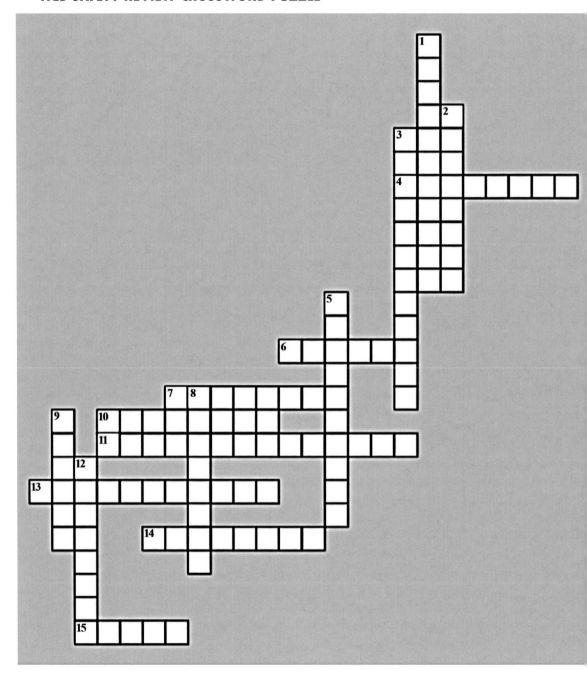

ACROSS

4. A specific string of letters, numbers, and characters to gain access to a website
6. An individual who uses computers to illegally gain access to information in computer systems
7. The anniversary of the day that a person was born
10. An online alias used to help identify a person
11. The act of providing proof of who you are
13. A physical characteristic that is unique to each individual
14. Specific characteristics of a person
15. Servers where personal information is stored via the internet

DOWN

1. Knowledge that you try to keep secure
2. The use of fake emails and websites to gain information such as usernames and passwords from people

3. Using letters and numbers

5. The practice of converting information to a code to prevent unauthorized access

8. Worldwide computer communications network

9. Portable, especially referring to a computer device

12. A system to aid memory using a phrase or code

REVIEW YOUR MOVES

• What other computer security terms can you think of?

• Use graph paper to make your own crossword puzzle.

• Can you make a crossword puzzle that also hides a secret message?

• How can you continue to improve your computer security skills as technology continues to change and improve?

TEACH YOUR GRANDMA TO BE SAFE!

 20–30 minutes

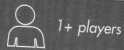 1+ players

YOUR MISSION

Despite using a computer all the time, nobody ever really thinks about digital security. Most people don't understand how to keep their information safe, how to decide if they can trust a website, why passwords should be complex, or why they shouldn't download unknown software. People who understand digital security—like you and your friends—have a responsibility to teach others why and how to keep their personal information safe!

Your Gear

- **Pencil**
- **Paper**

LET'S PLAY

Start off by grabbing some friends—you're going to work together to create a commercial to teach people about digital security. Now that you've assembled your team, everyone should think about the following:

- Choose a topic related to digital security. This could be something as simple as password strength or as complex as encrypted websites.

- Determine your audience. Will you be teaching your parents, friends, grandparents, or teachers?
- How can you explain the problem?
- What is the solution?
- Give a real-world example if you can!

Once you've got all that figured out, write the script for your commercial. Then, assign everyone a role to play. And of course, you'll all need to practice before your commercial goes live! Finally, perform your commercial for your intended audience or record your commercial to share with family and friends.

What Does the Internet Know About You?

In a digital world, stores and advertisers know much more about us than we might think. When you use a store loyalty card to get bonus points or discounts, you are paying for those benefits by sharing your personal information. Think about what your grocery store knows about you. By the amount of food you buy, it can probably figure out how many people are in your household. Are you buying food that would be considered kids' food? That's a good indication that there are children in the household. What about pets? Do you buy dog food, cat food, litter? Would your household be more likely to respond to advertising about new healthy, organic foods? Or might time-saving quick meals be better received?

REVIEW YOUR MOVES

• While you were coming up with your commercial, you probably learned something! The world of digital security is both huge and amazing.

• Think of how technology will evolve in the future. How will new technologies change the way you handle digital security?

ANSWER KEY

CAN YOU BREAK THE CODE? ANSWERS:

1. Use long passwords that have letters, numbers, and symbols.
2. Do not give anyone your personal information online or through text.
3. Do not download any unknown software.

BINARY MESSAGE DECODER ANSWERS:

The code reads: BINARY USES ONLY 0 AND 1

WORD SEARCH ENCRYPTED PASSWORD KEY ANSWERS:

1. encrypt: d
2. phish: e
3. mobile phone: c
4. password: r
5. hacker: y
6. firewall: p
7. virus: t
8. security: e
9. username: d

Hidden message: decrypted

WEB SAFETY REVIEW CROSSWORD PUZZLE ANSWERS:

ACROSS

4. password
6. hacker
7. birthday
10. username
11. identification
13. fingerprint
14. identity
15. cloud

DOWN

1. information
2. phishing
3. alphanumeric
5. encryption
8. internet
9. mobile
12. mnemonic

GLOSSARY

algorithm A specific and precise set of instructions, often used for a computer or program.

authenticate To confirm the truth of something.

binary Related to two things. The prefix "bi" means "two."

binary code A coding system that uses the digits 0 and 1 to represent other numbers, letters, or other characters.

bit The smallest unit of data in a computer code; the 0 or 1 in binary code is a bit.

breach A gap in a defense, such as a physical wall or the security protections of a website.

byte A string of bits in computer code, usually equal to eight bits. Computers nowadays can store many billions of bytes (gigabytes) or even a trillion bytes (a terabyte).

coding The act of writing computer programs using specific programming languages.

compromised Weakened, as data that has been hacked.

data Information in numerical form often used on computers.

deterrent Something that keeps or discourages something from occurring.

disclose To reveal.

encrypt To convert information using a code so that it can't be accessed unless someone has the code.

geolocation A method for finding the location of an online device anywhere on Earth.

mnemonic A pattern or device that helps people remember something.

phishing The practice of sending out fake emails to trick people into revealing personal information.

router A machine that directs the transfer of data from one network to another.

software Programs that a computer uses.

verification Process for checking the truth of something.

FURTHER READING

BOOKS

Kamberg, Mary-Lane. *Cybersecurity* (Digital and Information Literacy). New York, NY: Rosen Central, 2018.

La Bella, Laura. *Ciphers, Codes, Algorithms, and Keys*. New York, NY: Rosen Young Adult, 2017.

Selby, Nick, and Heather Vescent. *Tips for Your Personal Cybersecurity* (Cybersecurity Survival Strategies). New York, NY: Rosen Young Adult, 2019.

Shofner, Melissa. *Cybersecurity Expert* (Behind the Scenes with Coders). New York, NY: PowerKids Press, 2018.

WEBSITES

Break the Code
https://www.cia.gov/kids-page/games/break-the-code
Provides encryption activities, including one based on the Enigma code used in World War II.

Zuky's Safety Guide
https://www.paloaltonetworks.com/campaigns/kids-in-cybersecurity
A guide to cybersecurity with activities to test your knowledge.

INDEX